CASA MODERNA

HALF A CENTURY OF COLOMBIAN DOMESTIC ARCHITECTURE

CASA MODERNA

HALF A CENTURY OF COLOMBIAN DOMESTIC ARCHITECTURE

Director, designer and editor
BENJAMIN VILLEGAS

Research and written text
ALBERTO SALDARRIAGA
Professor, National University of Colombia

Photography
ANTONIO CASTAÑEDA BURAGLIA

Villegas
editores

This book has been created, produced and published
in Colombia by
© VILLEGAS EDITORES 1996
Avenida 82 No. 11-50, Interior 3
Telephone (57-1) 616 1788. Fax (57-1) 616 0020
Bogotá D.C., Colombia
e-mail: villedi@cable.net.co

www.villegaseditores.com

Editorial consultant
FRANCA PACINI

Layout
MERCEDES CEDEÑO

English translation
JIMMY WEISKOPF

Revised and corrected
ANGELA KERR

Supplementary photography
JOSE FERNANDO MACHADO, 89, 101, 186, 219.
PILAR GÓMEZ, 271, 272, 273.
CLAUDIA URIBE, 56, 57.
JORGE EDUARDO ARANGO 18, 88.
JEREMY HORNER, 179.
CARLOS TOBÓN, *Aló Casa,* 73.

Photographic assistant
HECTOR WIESNER

First Edition
November, 1996

Second Edition
November, 2001

ISBN 958-9393-24-1

The publisher wishes to express special thanks to
DAVIVIENDA
for having sponsored the first edition of this book.

Jacket, Bogotá, D.C., Architects, Fernando Martínez, Guillermo Avendaño
Back jacket, Cartagena, Bolívar. Architect, Rogelio Salmona
Pages 2/3, Arbeláez, Cundinamarca, Architect, Vicente Nasi.
Page 4, Bogotá, D.C., Architect, Carlos Campuzano.
Page 7, Cartagena, Bolívar, Architect, Rogelio Salmona.

FOREWORD

*C*asa Moderna develops the subject matter of a series of books which we have been publishing with the aim of spreading knowledge about the history of Colombian architecture from its earliest days to the creation of post-modernist houses.

With the publication of *Casa Colombiana*, the first in the series, we wanted to demonstrate tendencies in urban and rural domestic housing, paying tribute to the creativity of architects who sought to harmonize environment and climate with the characteristic building materials of their localities. Our research then led us to deal with an aspect of our architecture which had been ignored and merited revaluation: vernacular buildings, published in *Casa Campesina*. A further book, *Casa Colonial*, deals with a 300 year period during which the country experienced important changes. In the history of Colombian architecture no other epoch is so rich in innovations both in civil and religious architecture. The next book, called *Casa Republicana*, reveals the panorama of what is known as the *Belle Époque*, which lent a wealth of syncretisms and borrowings from foreign sources to our architecture.

Casa Moderna covers the second half of this century, from the end of the 1940s to the middle of the 1990s. With the invasion of modernism, fully illustrated in this book, a movement towards innovation and change imposes itself on the country, enriching contemporary Colombian architecture with surprising and attractive qualities which place it on a level with the world's most important schools of architectural thought, especially North American ones. But, despite these similarities, this architectural style has been the most vulnerable and ephemeral one in the country's history. Its brilliant destiny has been affected by a strange paradox: its houses, precursors of the country's urban progress, became the first victims of that progress. As these houses give way to buildings of larger dimensions, their fate casts doubt upon the possibilty of the conventional family-sized house's survival as a viable form of dwelling.

This book displays the best surviving examples of the architecture of the 1940s to the late 1960s, forerunners, in many aspects, of the most up-to-date developments in contemporary architecture which also help us to identity characteristic features of our urban culture. All of them being products, as well, of the imaginative work of our best Colombian architects.

BENJAMIN VILLEGAS

11

Left, The outer form of the house contradicts any predetermined image and announces some of the intentions which model the interior space. The sinuous line and solidity of the façade wall, with its irregular curvature and design, is lightly modified by some small openings.

Bogotá, D.C.

Architects, Fernando Martínez, Guillermo Avendaño.

PREAMBLE

The first modern house was built in Colombia some time between 1930 and 1940. No-one knows exactly where it was constructed. Its hypothetical presence, enables us to draw a line that separates the past from the present. From the moment it appeared, Colombian housing changed its orientation, abandoned its roots and turned wholeheartedly towards taking advantage of everything which modernism might offer to the country.

How does one distinguish a modern house from a traditional one? Its design must utilize a pure and unadorned geometry. Its building materials must be different from traditional ones. Its windows have to be considerably wider and allow the entrance of light and sun into the interior rooms. The concept of spaces is also applied in a different manner. Instead of an excessive subdivision into small enclosures, broader and intercommunicating spaces are favored. Instead of excessive ornamentation and the use of curious details, there is an attempt at clean surfaces within a general sense of simplicity and sobriety. Form and space, technique and materials, efficiency and simplification all, of these must be present within the modern house.

The modern house was and is a special phenomenon. It has been, for decades, the tangible realization of the modernization of domestic life. It has also been the place where many of the guiding principles of everyday existence, set by the conditions of modern life, have been put to the test. Its cardinal virtues were —or had to be— hygiene, functionalism, efficiency, light, and the absence of superfluous adornments. It must have no unusable spaces or dark corners. Everything must be clearly arranged so that life may be as easy and simple as possible. Sincerity in architecture must correspond to the sincerity of the ways of life. An abstract ordering is imposed on everyday living.

The modern house, as an independent unit, nowadays faces a very strong rival, the apartment, that space which is functionally incorporated within the interior of a building and suspended in the air. Nevertheless everyone speaks of "a house" when referring to the place where they live. The modern house is not a single thing. It adopts many different forms: the isolated house which is surrounded by its own setting, in the city or the country; the house which is delimited by walls of middling height which separate it from others; the house which is mass-produced in housing developments or complexes. The house is a social language. All of them exist in Colombia. This book is only a chapter in their description.

13

Left, Every one of the parts of the house has a meaning, given by its uses and contained in its forms. The intention of making a house into something that is nearly unique is precisely reflected in the handling of the forms which define space as one of its main characteristics.

Bogotá, D.C.
Architects, Fernando Martínez,
Guillermo Avendaño.

MODERN LIFE, MODERN HOUSE

Nothing is so obvious and so ambiguous as the modern. We recognize and experience, many things as modern, without necessarily understanding what modernism is; that way of thinking, acting and living which has marked world existence since at least the two centuries. The signs of the modern are easier to identify than the thought which upholds it. The sociologist Peter Berger summarizes this problem in the following way:

…"there are at least two aspects of modernity which place it in a special category, at least in the minds of intellectuals and probably in those of broader social groups as well. One is the assumption that modernity is not only different from, but also superior to all that preceded it. The other is the large number of individuals who presume they know authoritatively what modernity is all about"…[1]

According to the first of the hypotheses set forth by Berger, to be modern is to find oneself in the last and most advanced stage of human progress, understood as the accumulation of advances in science, technology, economy, politics, culture and everday life. To be modern is, or at least should be, to have at one's disposal all of those advances in order to reach the highest quality of life historically possible. This, obviously, cannot fail to be a theoretical assumption, a wish, which is far from expressing itself in an effective reality.

Marshall Berman, in his now classic book entitled *Todo lo sólido se desvanece en el aire*, refers to the modern in a different way:

"To be modern is to find ourselves in a setting that promises us adventure, power, happiness, growth, transformation of the self and of the world, and which, at the same time, threatens to destroy all that we own, all that we know, all that we are. Modern surroundings and experiences cross all frontiers of geography and race, class and nationality, religion and ideology. It can be said, in this sense, that modernity unites all of humanity. But it is a paradoxical unity, the unity of disunity: it throws us all into a whirlpool of perpetual disintegration and renewal, of struggle and contradiction, of ambiguity and anguish. To be modern is to form part of a universe in which, as Marx said, 'all that is solid melts into air' ."[2]

Both Berger and Berman refer to the consciousness of being in the midst of something special, different, new. That consciousness, in the field of intellect, refers to matters of knowledge, history, society and culture. In the world of everyday life modernity becomes more concrete, visible and inhabitable; things are perceived in a different way. The

Left, The space of the hall faces, in the distance, the old barracks, which recall the military origin of the site. The austerity of the stone walls and the brick vault and floor enables us to grasp, with more clarity, the formal values of the space which they define. Something of the serenity of a medieval space, translated to the present thanks to a refined idea of design, seems to be recreated here.

Cartagena, Bolívar.

Architect, Rogelio Salmona.

15

modern, as thought, is somewhat different from the modern as a common mode of life, as a routine, as a fashion. The visible signs of modernity are those which make it accessible to the ordinary person, which allow him to take part in *progress*, this being understood as a complex of discoveries and gifts which make everyday life easier or richer.

One peculiarity of modern culture is summed up in the expression, *the tradition of the new*. Lisímaco Parra says the following about this:

"In 1959 the American critic, Harold Rosenberg, coined the lucky expression, 'the tradition of the new'; modernity has a tradition, but, in contrast to the traditionalism which tries to enclose sacrosanct and eternal values in a casket, the tradition which upholds the modern is that which assumed the role of the new in its historical moment. This tradition now means that continual effort or that continual 'game' of trying to understand, given that all of the stagnant and mouldy relations, with their retinue of beliefs and ideas that have been venerated for centuries, are broken; the new ones turn stale before becoming ossified. All that is static and stagnant fades away; all that is sacred is profaned, and in the end men are forced to serenely reflect upon the conditions of their existence and their mutual relationships." [3.]

The *tradition of the new* may be found in the higher spheres of cultural tradition, although it is also to be seen in more prosaic fields. The association between the modern and the new is present in everyday life and expresses itself in the fever of novelty, which is mainly represented by the multiple varieties of fashion. To be modern and to be fashionable have become synonymous in the heart of contemporary cultures. Novelty is the indispensable requirement for being up to date.

Modernity became visible through the transformation of cities and buildings. A new spatial order, different from the traditional one, imposed itself as the real scenario of the new way of life. Urbanism and architecture were, initially, instruments to demonstrate the existence of that modern world and were later assumed to be an integral part of what modern life might be like. The image of Manhattan with its skyscrapers became the symbol of modernization and progress and the paradigm of the modern city. The skyscraper and the shopping centre were the new secular temples of the ordinary man and replaced the temples and palaces of the past.

The modernization of architecture has expressed itself, above all, in two different but interrelated fields. The first includes advances in the techniques of construction.

The second is made up of basic ideas about space and form. The technological changes which were initiated in the

19th century and became more fully developed in the 20th century influenced these abstract ideas about space and form and partly helped to make them more precise. The use of materials like concrete, iron, steel and glass became, at a certain time, a synonym for progress. The proposals about form and space formulated in the early decades of the 20th century were based on the idea of that technical progress and, on the basis of this recognition, were guided towards aesthetic explorations and spatial conceptions in accordance with the *spirit* of the modern.

The epithet of modern in architecture does not only arise from the physical qualities of spaces and buildings. The correct use of this term requires that it be placed within a specific context defined by the so-called "modern movements" and, particularly, the avant-garde manifestos and, programs of the turn of the century and the concrete examples of those programs. The quantity and different names of these modern movements (or of the Modern Movement, as the group is generically known) include such diverse proposals as those of Dutch Neo-Plasticism, Italian Rationalism, German Expressionism, Scandinavian and American Organicism and, above all, Functionalism as a variety of a universal tendency so influential that it has become a synonym of modernity for the ordinary person.

It is commonplace to say that modernization reached Colombia late in the day, that it has been a fragmented process, full of starts and turns and that the country today is not *completely* modern. In short, there exists in the country a juxtaposition of fragments of tradition and modern life, an amalgamation of those particular forms of culture and life characteristic of the countries which are in a state of perpetual transition or, as Néstor García Canclini puts it, of societies *"where traditions have not gone and modernization has not fully arrived."* [4.]

In contrast to the two great historical transformations which preceded it, the Spanish Conquest and the Independence, the modernization in Colombia, was not caused by unique factors, violent events or a brusque interruption of national life. By around 1930 there already existed many indications of modernization in the fields of politics, culture and economy in the daily life of some social minorities. The modernizing impulses were basically due to two objectives: that of progress in the political and economic spheres, and that of innovation in the cultural one. The ideal of progress adopted some of the strategies peculiar to that time: the modernization of state institutions, the development of new

business structures, an increase in industrial production, and the construction of a basic material infrastructure.

This innovation expressed itself in cultural changes and changes in day-to-day life. The new gradually became important. From that time onwards to be modern was –and perhaps still is– to be a bearer and advocate of the new. Progress was a sign of advancement, the new a sign of the contemporary.

The influence of the United States in the process of modernization in Colombia was decisive and began, at that time, to displace the cultural influence of France and England, which had been the ruling one ever since the mid-nineteenth century.

While modernism had originated in Europe, the United States was the place where the effectiveness of the modern was most clearly demonstrated, especially through the wide dissemination of successful inventions. In the United States, a pragmatic and utilitarian society, modernism was not considered a matter of theory but one of action. There, more than anywhere else, the concrete forms which would come to represent "modern life" reached their fullest expression. The telegraph, the telephone, the phonograph, the automobile, the airplane, the radio, cinema, photography and the skyscraper originated or became widely available in American society. *Mass culture* found a fertile field for its growth and multiplication. To be modern, around 1930, was a synonym for adopting everything which the American way of life made accessible, from the *foxtrot* to mass production.

Adopting the modern way of life was not easy in a country like Colombia, which had a conservative and traditionalist spirit that, around 1930, showed a notable backwardness in cultural, social and economic matters. Once the initial prejudices were overcome, the modern became obligatory and thereafter almost became a religion, reaching a point where everything to do with the past was seen as undignified, dirty and unpleasant. This process was a surprisingly rapid one, given the conditions just mentioned. In less than twenty years, the modern had become fashionable and was considered the best form of habitat for the population and, as a result, traditional forms of housing were rejected. Within this ambit, some social groups adopted modern tastes and customs and transformed the places where they lived in order to live in a modern way but without discarding their traditionalist or conservative mentality. The "fashionable" character given to the modern, the establishment of the tradition of the new which contributed to its spread around the world, helped establish, in Colombia, a

Left, The symmetry of the enormous space of the room gives it a certain air of grandeur, which is accentuated by the play of lines in the bamboos which form the elaborate structure of the roof. In the background these lines form a pattern which reason for being appears to have more to do with aesthetic than structural considerations.

Manizales, Caldas.
Architect, Simón Vélez.

timely modernization whose fragmented nature has still not been overcome.

Political and economic modernization necessarily found an expression in cities, buildings, and housing as well. Modern architecture entered Colombia as a symbol of progress and of novelty. The intellectual importance of the modern European movements and the curiosity aroused by the buildings and ways of life peculiar to the United States impelled its adoption in the country. Even though contacts between the country and the rest of the world were not very solid, the new ideas became known, professional training increased, and new entities and enterprises were created to put them into practice. Europe was the intellectual metropolis, the United States the source of concrete models.

The modernization of the cities and of architecture in Colombia has been a large and fragmented process. Towards the end of the past century a moderate change in construction techniques, which up to then had clung to colonial traditions, had already begun. Brick gradually replaced adobe and iron was used for small details and in a few structures of some magnitude: the Colón Theatre in Bogotá and the Heredia Theatre in Cartagena. Glass had already become commonplace and people were beginning to think about the possibility of using large windows. During the early decades of the present century the use of reinforced concrete spread, thanks to the development of the cement industry. It is thought that the first building constructed in reinforced concrete in the country was the Magdalena Hotel, in Puerto Berrío, Antioquia. In 1923 the Pedro A. López building, designed by an American architect, Robert M. Farrington, was constructed in Bogotá. Its structure, in *cement and steel, according to the American style*[5], is not revealed by the neo-classical style of its façade. Between 1925 and 1930 various buildings which used new construction techniques were built in the principal cities of the country. The introduction and development of new spatial and formal concepts took place betwen 1930 and 1940. The hypothetical origin of the modern Colombian house is situated in that decade.

The first modern ideas about urbanism and architecture reached Colombia, in a fragmentary way, in the nineteen-thirties, together with the stylistic influences of *Art-Deco*, which, at that time, had a world influence as a brief pre-modern interlude. It is probable that many houses were first built in this style before the construction of our hypothetical first modern house, whose traces are practically impossible to find. The modern image of the Colombian house was designed on the basis of those principles of simplification and functionalism and from the beginning was associated with the idea of new furnishing and a new concept of objects.

The new house, which hypothetically appeared between 1930 and 1940, completely broke with the traditional image of republican houses and, even more, with that of colonial houses. The purity of forms, the absence of ornament, the simplicity of the enclosures, the interest in light reflected in the use of large windows, all of this was radically different from the ornamented half-lit corners of the republican and the rustic spaces of the colonial. To make this house work, a new furnishing, a new equipping was necessary. A piece of antique furniture might look completely anachronistic in it. The modernization of domestic space had to be an integral act. It was also necessary to have a new kind of city.

In a book entitled *Arquitectura en Colombia*, published in 1951 by the architects Jorge Arango and Carlos Martínez, the best of the architectural work done between 1946-1951 was presented, for the first time, in a condensed version. In an aside entitled "The Background of Contemporary Architecture", the following optimistic commentary is to be found:

"It is not surpising that, with the great economic development which Colombia had between 1935 and 1950, a wish to renew buildings should appear and that the fever of renovation in the cities should coincide with the interests of its young architects." [6.]

The transformation of Colombian cities was neither immediate nor complete. A great part of early modern architecture was constructed in city centres, in properties where the existing buildings were being demolished. During a certain period of time modern building preceded the first concrete results of modern urbanism, which only expanded after 1950. The properties of the historic centres of the cities were not really adequate for the initiatives of this architecture: it was only in the new residential neighborhoods that the ideal conditions for its development were to be found. For this reason, it was only in the new urbanism that the modern Colombian house could find its full expression.

The modern housing developments were fashioned on the basis of relatively common assumptions that were applicable to all levels of society. The property or building lot had to be lengthened towards the inner part of the block, with a smaller front and a greater depth. In high-income neighborhoods these properties were large enough to allow for the establishment of some rather simple urban norms: the building should occupy the front of the lot, while most of the interior part should be the garden. The roominess of the

dimensions of these neighborhoods favored the building of one-storey houses, whose sides –or nearly all of them– were isolated from neighboring ones. In neighborhoods destined for social groups with lower incomes the idea, from the beginning, was to build two-storey houses, between party walls. For this reason, the one-storey house was, for many years, a symbol of social prestige and the best representative of the modern idea of the house.

One of the things which distinguished the first modern houses from their predecessors was the concept of functional distribution. The interior of the house was organized in line with criteria of zoning in accordance with the three main functional groups: the social zone (living room, dining room, study), the private zone (bedrooms and bathrooms), and the service zone (kitchen, laundry room, maid's room, garage). The old-fashioned vestibule or closed *hall* gave way to a space of functional distribution to which all of the zones had or at least should have had access. A correct functional arrangement was the basic condition of any attempt at a truly modern house.

In addition to a correct functional arrangement and an advanced construction technique, the spatiality of the modern house is that which most characterizes it and distinguishes it from the preceding one. In broad terms, it is possible today to speak of two different conceptual and spatial tendencies in the modern Colombian house which give evidence of two distinct interpretations of the meaning of modernity in architecture. The first and most abstract of these has been marked by a spatiality which is as neutral as possible, faithfully following functional lineaments as the generating principles of the house design. The other, which is obviously different, favors the search for a strong interrelation between the inside and outside of the dwelling and attempts a spatial characterization through the use of such resources as the texture of the building materials, changes in height and management of light. In historical terms, the first of these spatial ideas preceded the appearance of the second and this left a definitive mark on the general character of Colombian architecture.

In a second book entitled *Arquitectura en Colombia*, published in 1963, architect Carlos Martínez described the new residential architecture in the following terms:

The new residences are characterized by a different order in the location of the living spaces, by simpler adornments, by the use of glass in profusion, together with materials whose textures and tones are made more evident. Innumerable houses are being constructed nowadays with such splendid finishings, such modern

23

Left, The circulations of the house are spaces which, when given a value, acquire a special importance. The lobby is dominated by the light which enters through the glass canopy. Its link with the porch is made into a pretext for the forming of a solid brick cylinder which takes on a certain sculptural quality.

Tenjo, Cundinamarca.
Architects, Willem Goebertus,
Catalina Mariño.

installations in their bathrooms and kitchens and such a variety of comforts in their main rooms, that they might be considered an unobtainable aspiration for families in an elevated economic position in more advanced countries."[7.]

The above description coincides with what one might expect of a dwelling projected and constructed in the terms characteristic of the functional and rational thought of European architecture in the first half of the century. The analogy of the house as a *machine for living*, formulated in 1923 by the Swiss architect, Le Corbusier and initially applied to "economical", practical and functional houses, was proposed as the model of new way of living. That famous analogy, one of the commonplaces of early modern architecture, was not a formal matter: the idea was never to make houses in the same way that one makes an apparatus. The problem mainly referred to the understanding of the space of a residence as a complex of functions which were efficiently joined to one another, with the minimum of wasted space. This house could not, in any way, lodge heavy and inefficient furniture and objects: it was necessary to design new kinds of furniture and objects for it. Every new house had to be a reason for experimenting with the possibilities of the new ways of living.

The house as a machine for living was the ideal of functionalism, and this is difficult to define in a precise way. It was an analagous concept whose concrete expression was the distribution of the different spaces of the building in such a way that the relations of use would be carried out in an efficient way and without interferences. The aesthetic problem of this new house could not have been resolved by means of analogy. But by around 1930 the new language of architecture had already advanced notably. Adolf Loos had published, in 1910, his polemical text entitled *Ornament and Offence*, in which he severely criticized the ornamental fever of the *Belle Époque* and advocated the search for simplification, which he himself set out to demonstrate through a series of projects in which a bare geometry, directly voiced, served as support for smooth and colorless designs, devoid of moulding. The Dutch movement, *De Stijl* or *Neo-Plasticism*, had published, in 1917, a manifesto in which the plane was held to be the creating element of all architecture. Le Corbusier had already sketched out, around 1920, his purist language and the German *New Objectivity* movement had defined many of the principles of the new rationalism. All of these tendencies came, in some way, to influence the modern Colombian house.

Germán Téllez refers, in the following terms, to what he labels the *architectural catechism* of the nineteen fifties:

"The exterior must reflect the organization of the interior. The structure must be expressed in a direct way, without any kind of decorative treatment. Openings in the façade must predominate over any other functional or compositional element. Space is only measured and understood on the basis of simple prismatic volumes of right-angles. All architecture, in order to be beautiful in design and adequate in volume, must have short and clear circulating areas and contiguous ones exclusively dictated by functional or mechanical conveniences. The new materials and techniques of construction will be accepted and employed without any questioning, independently of their convenience or economy." [8.]

A look at some of the houses built between 1950 and 1960 shows a wide range of interpretation of the rationalist paradigm modified by a notable imagination. The new house had to represent all of that which was paradigmatically modern. In this way the break with the past and interest in the present was clearly shown. This spirit is evident in the earliest houses designed by the architects Vicente Nasi and Gabriel Serrano, two of the pioneers in the modernization of housing in Colombia. They were joined by such outstanding architects as Jorge Arango, Alvaro Ortega, Gabriel Solano, Bruno Violi, and Gabriel Lagarcha, and some firms which were responsible for a particularly significant residential architecture in the period betwen 1950 and 1960.

The houses constructed by the firm Obregón Valenzuela and Company, mostly designed by the architect Rafael Obregón, may be considered as some of the most representative of that first modern spirit. With clear functionalist roots and the aesthetic influences of such personalities as Richard Neutra and Mies van der Rohe, the houses of Obregón Valenzuela were, in their time, the most polished examples of the new Colombian domestic architecture. Pretty much the same can be said about the houses designed, in that same period, by the firms Ricaurte Carrizosa Prieto and Triana Vargas Rocha in Bogotá and by Lago Sáenz and Borrero Zamorano Giovanelli in Cali. Geometrically rigorous, these modern houses were worked as abstract compositions, with a clear separation of functional zones, a rational design which allowed for impeccable construction, a skilful handling of horizonal and vertical planes and of closings and openings, and with a careful treatment of all details. Few of these houses have survived and those which have survived have been modified to the point of being unrecognizable.

The welcome given to these new habitational forms was surprising and rapid. Between 1950 and 1960 to be modern became fashionable. The modernizing interest permeated

practically all of the urban social groups and a notorious transformation in the physical structure of cities took place, occasioned by the expansion of the areas of housing on the peripheries of the historic centres. Apart from the houses designed by architects, modern houses erected by builders and construction workers also appeared. The centuries-old lag in construction techniques rapidly gave way to a boom in concrete buildings with metallic window-frames, diverse renderings in the façades and an unequivocally modern appearance.

The abstract period of the Colombian house did not last for more than two decades. The debates about architecture at the end of the nineteen-fifties raised doubts about the validity of the foundations of this functionalist-abstract movement. New alternatives appeared and new possibilities were opened.

"The setting, the landscape, the functionally necessary volumes are the elements of base which, when organized, are going to create, on the one hand, this intentional space and, on the other, the integration of the whole to the setting. The filling of exterior space is not limited, therefore, by the space itself, instead, it prolongs it within a general space, immediately creating an architectural landscape starting from a reality: the existing landscape and the lyrical base - the different spaces between the volumes." [9.]

With those words, written about a project done by Fernando Martínez Sanabria, the architect Rogelio Salmona set forth, in 1959, what would be the manifesto of a change in architecture and in the attitude of some professionals with regard to the functionalist tendencies which, by that time, had become institutionalized as the most representative of modern architecture. The change originated and was developed in Bogotá and later extended to other cities in the country. Its principles were influenced by what was called *organic* architecture, in accordance with the terminology then current in the international debate and were especially shaped by the ideas of the Italian historian Bruno Zevi, who was, at that time a radical opponent of functionalism. The architectural paradigm for this movement was, initially, that of the U.S. architect Frank Lloyd Wright and the Finnish Alvar Aalto. Later on, the influence of the work of Louis Kahn became definitive.

The historian Silvia Arango relates the birth of this architectural movement in the following way:

"Although its beginnings were marginal and limited to small circles in Bogotá, the evolution of the topological movement in the decade of the 60's later became very important. The original ideas of this movement, when they were formulated at the end of the

27

Left, The house's response to the climate allows for work with water, light and shadow, the enclosed and the open, as signs of that which it seeks to offer: heat and coolness, dryness and moisture, darkness, and light. All of this provides an opportunity for strong contrasts which emphasize the image of the "hot climate".

Ricaurte, Cundinamarca.

Architect, Jorge Pérez Norzagaray.

nineteen fifties, tended to be identified, in a confused way, with 'organicism', meaning formal liberty, curved lines, intricate spaces and integration with the surrounding nature. Within a world panorama, having passed through the conceptual sieve of Bruno Zevi, the movement towards an "architecture of place", conscious of geography and local materials, seemed to be best represented by Wright and perhaps Aalto. Zevi's interpretation of Wright and his emphasis on the particularity of space and the "organicist" ideology would be widely accepted and spread by certain academic circles. By the middle of the nineteen sixties, for example, "Saber ver la arquitectura" was one of the few textbooks bought by students. Given the precarious nature of national theoretical efforts, the theories of Zevi came to meet the analytical needs of a group which anxiously sought conceptual supports for their intuitions about design. Nevertheless, these initial ideas would soon turn out to be insufficient and furthermore, the pressure exercised by local realities would force into existence a conceptual and architectural development more suitable to the country." [10.]

The enthusiasm awakened by this new approach to architecture became contagious among a whole generation of brilliant professionals who lived in Bogotá and spread, in a lesser degree, to professionals who resided in other cities, in which the rational spirit persisted for a longer time. The Bogotá house was, therefore, for several years, the most representative of this new conception of architecture and it became a paradigm whose influence is still felt in Colombia. On the basis of this change of direction a fruitful stage of searching for spatial and formal alternatives came into being, which expressed itself through the handling of materials that were at hand, especially brick and wood. The house was one of the preferred fields of exploration. In the house forms and spaces different from those already established in the functionalist language were experimented with. Out of these experiments there later arose the idea of the *architecture of place*, a term which indicates a sense of space which goes beyond the merely functional.

Some doubts about and outbreaks of rebellion against the models which were already established and formalized just then became evident in Colombian professional circles towards the end of the nineteen seventies. The coincidence between these doubts and the rise of post-modern ideas about architecture and culture in general was not completely accidental. The decade of the seventies was a time of general questioning in all fields. The recognition of the *other* cultures was significant. This led to the revaluation of the architectural heritage and of vernacular architectures, with their spatial concepts which were different and, in a certain way, distant from the modern idea about space. At the same time, a consciousness of the Latin American as a phenomenon worthy of attention and analysis was established.

The architecture of the house in the past two decades has had, as a point of reference, the affirmation or denial of what was proposed between 1950 and 1970. Criticism of modernity and especially of functionalism has favored the appraisal of the architecture of place as an important expression full of interesting elements. A scrutiny of the avant-garde of the first modern architecture has, in a parallel fashion, allowed for the recuperation of its formal principles. The encounter with tradition has made room for spatial and technical experiments which try to elaborate, with new ideas, that which has an unrealized potential. And, what is more significant, new generations of professionals have shown, through their work, their own attitudes towards architecture and, especially, towards the subject of the house.

A retrospective look at the development of the modern house in Colombia allows us to clearly see the counterpoint which grew up around the contrast between the abstract, functional, and rational approach and the *organic* approach sensitive to the environmental and spatial qualities of the place. This dualism, which has been resolved, at times, by polarities and, at times, by synthesis, definitively marked and still marks the modest story of the modern house in Colombia. The best examples show, as they always have done, the talent and sensibility of those who take charge of, design and bring to realization that transcendental commitment to construct the spaces that others live in.

The modern Colombian house has changed its location. Many of the new houses that are being built in Colombia are to be found in suburban areas, in places relatively distant from the historic centres and neighborhoods that were important around 1950. The houses of the past are no longer only republican and colonial ones but also many of the first modern houses. Today, when the idea of post-modernity has reached its summit, the paradigm of the modern house persists and exercises an influence on that which is being built every day. To speak of a post-modern house is something which is still a bit vague, just as the discussion about the beginning and end of modernity is vague. The *spirit of the epoch*, thought, at the beginning of the century, to be a support for the new architecture, has been replaced today by a swarm of spirits from different epochs and different places. The modern house is influenced by all of them.

SPACE AND FORM

The problem of form is essential for an understanding of the modern house. In contrast to the traditional house, whose forms were given legitimacy by cultural values and the utility of having established norms, in the modern house form arises from the rationalism and the imagination of the architect. There are not –or there should not be– any preconceived forms; one only makes use of a geometry which allows for the shaping of all which reason and imagination make possible. In the rationalist approach, the Cartesian grid defines all of the formal possibilities and sub-divisions of space. In the organic approach this grid is eliminated and a sequence of forms juxtaposed into space is created. The first is obvious and precisely follows what is proposed. The second is complex and requires a travelled movement to capture the richness of the proposed space.

The modern house as a problem of form and space had one of its best expressions in the domestic architecture of Fernando Martínez Sanabria, who constructed in Bogotá between 1960 and 1970. His work was based on the sense of adapting a property in order to gain control of all which might lend value to the interior space. This was conceived as a consequence of everything relating to the premises of design: topographic levels, near or distant views, inter-relations between the spaces, intentionally-sought directions. The outer wrapping of the house, fashioned with a clear sense of volumetric unity, shelters an interior space which is rich in perspective, movement and visual grace. A special geometry, skilfully managed, allowed for the consolidation of these intentions.

Several houses built in Bogotá between 1959 and 1965 form what might be considered as the architectural manifesto of Fernando Martínez. In each one of them, constructed in different terrains and conditions, the architect proposed and resolved a series of problems of interior spatiality in relation to the site and the volumes. Without abandoning the careful spatial arrangement of the functional areas of the dwelling, inherited from his previous rationalist period, Martínez explored, in these houses, such spatial resources as curved and winding walls, changes in level, strongly inclined roofs, void inter-communicating interiors, openings functionally arranged around near and distant views, and the aesthetic possibilities of a few basic materials: brick for the exterior, white-painted plaster, and wood in the interior. Brick, in his own words, was especially apt for the formation

Left, The work of the walls and roofs define, in principle, the form of the domestic space. But it is the elaboration of the interior surfaces and volumes which gives it a particular and unique character. Texture and color help to arrange that which will serve as background and that which will stand out as form, so that the total image of the architecture of the house may be created.

Bogotá, D.C.

Architect, Rafael Obregón.

31

of the large, closed exterior planes, absent of any ornamentation and perforated by some small openings towards the street. A study of the details was an indispensable part of the originality of each house. The architecture of the houses of Fernando Martínez, a special case in modern Colombian architecture, is exceptional from every point of view. Two aspects deserve a special mention. The first of these is the intention of integrating the interior space through a play of levels, voids, ceiling profiles, and spaces opened in the walls in the manner of windows. The second is the breaking of conventional geometric schemes and the free handling of unusual lines –curves and diagonals– which uphold the will to integrate and act as directional signals for the interior movements and the visual effects towards the outside. All of it realized within a rather ascetic handling of the materials and colors.

The architecture of the houses of Fernando Martínez is different, both conceptually and aesthetically, to the domestic architecture designed by Rafael Obregón and brought into being by his firm, Obregón Valenzuela and Company. The fact of having always worked through his company has blurred the importance of this eminent architect, one of the most solid in his ideas of architecture and one of the most rigorous in his execution. Germán Téllez talks about Obregón in the following way: *"Trained in the United States, Obregón and other colleagues of his generation, brought a new, diaphanous and clear architecture to Colombia, but one without stylistic mystery or malice and as far-removed from the hard realities of the country as it is possible to imagine. Skillfully softening it, they implanted it in our environment and the gospel preached in other latitudes by the European masters exiled in the United States –Gropius, Breuer, Neutra and others– flourished in Colombia. Little by little Colombian architecture became internationalized, abandoning the eclecticism of the previous years."* [11.]

Rafael Obregón explored sources that were different from those of Fernando Martínez. His paradigms were, as Germán Téllez says, the great masters of the functionalist and rationalist movement which had established itself in the United States during the nineteen fifties. His interest in studying Japanese architecture influenced his ideas about his own house, a perfect example of simplicity and sobriety, with generous spaces arranged in a sequential way and inter-communicated by means of glass screens or sliding doors. This house, by virtue of its overwhelming modernity, was one of the first examples of Colombian architecture to be featured in foreign publications.

In the same decade, the sixties, the architect Guillermo Bermúdez Umaña designed and built a series of houses in which he set forth his own idea of the organic: an asymmetrical composition of stories, a concept of volume which differentiated each of the zones of the house and, above all, that sense of interior space and relation to the setting, which is characteristic of the idea of place. His own house, designed in 1952, anticipated these ideas, which were proposed in a language very close to that of rationalism. The domestic architecture of Guillermo Bermúdez has its own special development, characterized by a clear sense of detail and the belief in a total architecture.

The historian Carlos Niño refers to the domestic architecture of Bermúdez in the following way: *"In the first case (the individual house) the approach adopted by the architect is that of an introverted development towards a private interior space and a drastic negation of the public street, generally speaking, a source of all kinds of irritating impositions. The façades towards the street are closed walls, which are only perforated at the points of entrance and with openings that are strictly indispensable. Towards the interior the concept is completely opposite, with façades treated on the basis of large windows which establish that interior-exterior permeability with transitional terraces, a constant feature of his work. The design is centrifugal, around a nuclear entrance space. In the cases of relatively small terrains, a concept of right-angle organization rules. When the terrains are more extensive, which applies to large mansions, the bodies of construction freely spread out from the centre through the park like giant fingers, and the roofs take pride in covering the whole like a great mantle."* [12.]

The houses designed by Fernando Martínez and Guillermo Bermúdez represent a theoretical and practical break with the rationalist approach which had characterized the spirit of the nineteen fifties and which had been exemplified by the houses designed by Rafael Obregón, Bruno Violi, and other architects. Following this rupture diverse alternatives arose, some more and others less inclined to each of the two opposing groups. A third alternative arose and is still seen in a domestic architecture which chooses a certain balance between the two extremes. The architecture of Enrique Triana Uribe, who worked for a number of years in association with Santiago Vargas Rocha, demonstrates the transition between the initial sober rationalism and a later synthesis in which deliberate details alternate with a rigorous geometrical design of the project.

The co-existence of diverse approaches, especially the architecture of abstraction and of place, defined as the main guides of the modern Colombian house, lasted till the present.

Left and above, The first
modern house? Perhaps not.
But it is a masterpiece of the
first domestic architecture
conceived in modern terms
in the country: clarity and
firmness in the handling of
volumes, each according to
its functional content; a
skilful management of
geometry; a clear intention
of contrast with surrounding
nature and a masterly
control of all of the
architectural details.

Arbeláez, Cundinamarca.
Architect, Vicente Nasi.

Left and above, A deliberate contrast is made between the exterior of the house, with its strong texture of brick visible, and the smooth white surfaces of the interior.

Fine wooden lines emphasize the borders of the jambs and railings. A contrapuntal play is also created between the sculpted volume of the stairway, the curve of the upper railing, the diagonal of the lower railing, and the right-angledness of the openings.

Bogotá, D.C.
Architects, Fernando Martínez,
Guillermo Avendaño.

Above and right, Even when, by definition, every dwelling has an interior space, this is rarely considered to be a matter of design. In this house a set of visual directions, of direct and indirect relations and plays of level and height are set forth, all of them sustained by the handling of the walls and hollows. The ceiling is conceived of as one of the main elements which give form to the space of the house.

Bogotá, D.C.
Architects, Fernando Martínez, Guillermo Avendaño.

Above, right and following pages, The exterior volume of the house is almost hermetic. Its geometry defines the main characteristics of the interior space, whose treatment is austere but suggestive at the same time. The idea of continuity is shown in the break-down of edges, in the joining of surfaces, in the curvature of the ceiling and also in the sequence of visual effects in different places of the house.

Bogotá, D.C.
Architects, Fernando Martínez, Guillermo Avendaño.

41

44

Above, The communication between the enclosures is not only a question of access or connection, it is also an aesthetic problem. The threshold opened in the wall serves as a kind of frame to enclose the interior view. The contrasting play of different geometries is appreciated, together with the strong sense of directionality which they give to the space of the house.

Bogotá, D.C.
Architects, Fernando Martínez, Guillermo Avendaño.

45

Above, The interior architecture of the house might be defined as "the wise and magnificent play of light upon the walls".
Each of the walls which interact in this space has a different form and character. One of them is broken to become both railing and furniture. Another opens in order to give way to the adjacent area. A third, which is completely closed, acts as a background.

Bogotá, D.C.
Architects, Fernando Martínez, Guillermo Avendaño.

Left, An aperture, technically speaking, is any opening that is made in a wall. In aesthetic terms, an aperture is a presence with a poetic character which converts a space and a few figures into the subject of a picture.

Bogotá, D.C.
Architects, Fernando Martínez,
Guillermo Avendaño.

49

Left and above, The form of the space is the shaping of a void. Making this form evident, as in this house, is achieved thanks to the clarity given to the definition of each of the elements of the confines: the walls, the floor, and the roof. Seen as an abstraction, the house is understood as a composition of straight and curved lines, solid and transparent planes, different textures and subtle changes of coloration. The surrounding light brings out the linear composition of a railing.

Bogotá, D.C.
Architect, Guillermo Bermúdez Umaña.

50

Above, The conscious handling of the formal values of each component of the interior space of the house allows for the creation of defined planes, whose proportions are intentional and not an accidental result. The monochromatic character and neutrality of white, a favorite color in the domestic architecture of the nineteen sixties, is only altered by the dark coloring of the floor.
Each surface is worked in the most perfect way possible.

Bogotá, D.C.
Architect, Guillermo Bermúdez Umaña.

51

Above, The study of the scale of the spaces leads to the introduction of alterations and contrasts in form and height, without losing sight of what might be called the "exact proportion of the domestic". The somewhat unusual presence of polished wooden beams in the space of the hall suggests a memory of the ancestral. The window introduces the garden to the enclosure, allowing it to participate in the interior life of the house.

Bogotá, D.C.
Architect, Guillermo Bermúdez Umaña.

53

Left and above, The conceptual differentiation between the exterior, as a sculptured mass, and the interior, as a purposely-moulded void, is made evident in a precise way. There is reciprocity in the working of the exterior volumes and the working of the surfaces of the walls and roof in the interior. By virtue of its sobriety and absence of color, this interior is perceived as an exercise in pure abstraction.

Funza, Cundinamarca.
Architect, Guillermo Bermúdez Umaña.

54

Above and right, The lines of
the roof give rise to a play of
surfaces which are broken in
various directions. The
monochromaticism softens
these intersections
while the light contradicts
this effect and creates
contrasts which give an

individual identity to each
plane. The cylinder adds a
different element to the
rectilinear geometry of the
whole.

Funza, Cundinamarca.
Architect, Guillermo Bermúdez
Umaña.

Left and above, The increase in the scale of space gives it a bigger role to play and reduces the importance of the furnishing. The almost symmetrical division of the background plane into two halves, one transparent and the other solid, determines the meaning and the character of the two zones. The ceiling, worked in the form of a complex ensemble of surfaces, guides the spatiality towards the big window which faces the garden.

Medellín, Antioquia.
Architect, Guillermo Bermúdez Umaña.

57

58

Above, right and following pages, An obvious relation exists between the elongated proportions of the window and the distant horizontal of the edge of the lake. The transparent plane is filled with the texture of the landscape and leads it to the interior. The inclined slope of the roof and the lesser height of the window direct one's glance towards this border and lead it on towards the distance. The effect is poetical.

Paipa, Boyacá.
Architect, Guillermo Bermúdez Umaña.

63

Left and above, The windows are transparent walls which, at the same time, close and open the interior space towards the landscape. The fireplace bursts forth with strength, determining different ambits without completely separating them. The elaborate wood work of the ceiling follows the forms of the house both in its floor-plan and volume.

Bogotá, D.C.
Architect, Rafael Obregón.

Left, A liking for natural materials has, for decades, been a constant feature in the architecture of the modern house in Colombia. Ceramic tiles, wood and smooth, white-painted walls were and still are a sign of sobriety. The way in which the forms are worked in space and the changes of direction give character to the interior of the house and accentuate the purely architectural interest of the project.

Bogotá, D.C.

Architect, Rafael Obregón.

66

Above and right, The white architecture of the interior of the house, the amplitude of the spaces, the plays on height and the dominant presence of the ceiling are characteristics of an architectural tendency in the Bogotá house. There is, in it, something of the abstraction of the colonial tradition and, especially, of its spirit of austerity.

Bogotá, D.C.
Architect, Rafael Obregón.

68

Above and right, A modern house in a warm climate is liberated from the need to have permanent closures and is designed as a big roof which gives shade to freely integrated spaces with an exterior which is only defined by the protection which it offers. The water of the swimming pool, next to the house, is a scaled down replica of the water in the marine landscape. The idea is one of transparency, freshness and light.

Cartagena, Bolívar.
Architect, Rafael Obregón.

70

Above, The traditional shelter
of the Caribbean Coast has
had, as its main function,
since bygone times, the giving
of shade and coolness. This
same intention is applied
here, in a modern language,
in order to obtain the same
results.

Barú, Bolívar.
Architect, Rafael Obregón.

Above, The closed planes
of this volume are
combined in an abstract
composition, rigorously
modern, that signals order
in the midst of the

asymmetry and
exuberance of the tropical
vegetation.

Barú, Bolívar.
Architect, Rafael Obregón.

72

Above and right, A sailboat is a floating house. Its outer forms obey the principles of navigation and the architect makes use of them in order to develop spaces for permanence and for activity. The deck, as a terrace, is the open "living room" of the craft whose outward beauty announces its agility and swiftness.

The term, "naval architecture", suggests the idea of big vessels. Here "an architecture for the sea" is more fitting.

Caribbean Sea.
Architect, Rafael Obregón.

74

Above, The interior space of the sailboat is a set of wise design choices. The need to integrate activities within the small internal space of the craft demands an exact handling of the dimensions of the elements, giving a specific function to each one of them in order to facilitate the comfort and mobility of the persons on board.

Caribbean Sea.
Architect, Rafael Obregón.

Above, In the interior of the sailboat the separation between furniture and space disappears. The working of different levels allows for the creation of sites for sitting and sleeping. The differences in height serve to create both back supports and storage space. The blue fabrics are an obvious and, at the same time, an affectionate reference to the sea, which is there, just outside.

Caribbean Sea.
Architect, Rafael Obregón.

Left and above, The white masses and forms of the volumes contrast with the ruggedness of the landscape. Memories of the architecture of the Mediterranean, evident in this case, accentuate the counterpoint between the forms, colors, and textures of the house and the rocks behind which it seems to want to hide itself. The balcony, supported by one of the rocks, offers a minimal incursion of geometry.

Santa Marta, Magdalena.
Architect, José María Obregón.

Above and right, The two faces of the space show a different treatment. Towards the front the rhythmically arranged vertical lines of the windows and the fireplace emphasize its height. Towards the background, the closed surfaces of the walls form cavities which are juxtaposed and whose use and furnishing provide different textures and colors.

Bogotá, D.C.
Architect, Enrique Triana Uribe.

80

Above and right, Scale, proportions, forms and textures, all that which forms part of the architecture of the house, are worked here in a special way. The architect expresses himself through intentions of quantity and quality. The handling of each material is joined to an interest in emphasizing the shape of every part, from the curves of the vault to the sculptural meaning of the fireplace.

Bogotá, D.C.

Architect, Roberto Rodríguez Silva.

82

Above, The rustic treatment
of some of the surfaces of
the interior of the house
formed part of the
experiments with texture
which were associated with
the idea of the modern house
in Colombia. The geometric
treatment of the stonework
indicates an intention to avoid
references to conventional
masonry.

Bogotá, D.C.
Architect, Alberto Manrique
Convers.

Right, The moulding of the
library ceiling is a clear
invocation of the colonial
past and proposes a contrast
with the modern lines and
surfaces of the rest of the
house. The texture and
coloring of the moulding
round off the general idea of
the space with its two
clearly-defined horizontal
strips.

Bogotá, D.C.
Architect, Francisco Pizano de
Brigard.

85

Left and above, A small courtyard inserted into the middle of the house provides views, illumination, and a transparerency which allows one to see other enclosures. Its reduced space favors a careful study of openings and closings.

In the interior, the play with the oblique lines of the railings and the ceiling intervenes in the right-angledness which generates the whole house.

Bogotá, D.C.
Architect, Cecilia Cifuentes de Caro.

Left and above, The earthen colors of the walls harmonize with the colors of the wood and soften the visual impact of the contrasts. The use of white in the frames of the doors and windows works in an opposite way. The intention of integrating spaces, evident in the interior treatment of this house, makes the lobby a literal "common place".

Bogotá, D.C.

Architect, Mauricio Samper.

88

Above, The integration between the two stories of the house is achieved, in a rather overwhelming way, through the use of ramps. The interior space of the house remains defined by those diagonals which invite one to make a real journey through it, one that is less direct and efficient, but richer in sensations than that offered by a stairway.

Manizales, Caldas.
Architect, Robert Vélez.

Above, The diagonal tension of the void, emphasized by the diagonals of the ramps, is visually neutralized by the work of the ceilings with the wooden stretches which separate the white boards and visually attracts attention. Wood dominates the whole and gives it a friendlier feeling.

Manizales, Caldas.
Architect, Robert Vélez.

90

Above and right, The house is conceived of as an abstract exercise in which elements as conventional as some stairs are incorporated as a simple succession of horizontal and vertical planes. The smooth or rough surfaces of the planes, their transparency or opaqueness, the polished, and the rustic surfaces are worked in order to give them a particular identity. The magnificent view is present throughout.

Cali, Valle del Cauca.
Architects, Manuel Lago, Jaime Sáenz.

92

Above and right, The
separation between the
vaulted roof and the interior
partitions of spaces, designed
as a function of the climate,
brings out the environmental
qualities of the house.
The simplification of the
architectural idea is
enriched by the working of
materials. One literally
breathes an air of freedom in
all the spaces.

Cali, Valle del Cauca.
Architect, Jaime Errázuriz.

PLACE AND TEXTURE

In contrast to the abstract logic of the functionalist idea, the house as place is a matter of sensibility. In every case it is a question of exploring the possibilities offered by a terrain: near and distant visual effects, topography, lighting, sunlight and ventilation, to the benefit of an interior space in which the walls, the voids and the profile of the roof which generates dynamic feelings. The peculiarity of the design of these houses is mainly reflected in their relation with the terrain and their surroundings and in the intentional handling of geometry to aid these effects. The textures of the materials which are worked give a tactile sense to the interior space, which, in the end, is the protagonist of the experience of the house.

The idea of the house as place took off at the beginning of the nineteen seventies, on the basis of the ideas advanced by the organicist movement. In its initial period which, in broad terms, occurred in the nineteen sixties, various professionals based in Bogotá, apart from Fernando Martínez, took an active part in its development: Dicken Castro, Hans Drew, Arturo Robledo, Rogelio Salmona, Reinaldo Valencia, and Hernán Vieco. Each one of them interpeted these ideas in his own way and expressed them in different projects, many of which were of fundamental importance for the subsequent development of Colombian architecture. A second generation of professionals broadened the field of possibilities for the house as place: Laureano Forero and Oscar Mesa en Medellín, Heladio Muñoz in Cali, Jacques Mosseri, Jorge Rueda, and Carlos Morales in Bogotá. A third and younger generation has developed these ideas, refuting or affirming them and, as the heirs of an architectural movement, this generation manages it at its own discretion and brings it up to date through the incorporation of new elements.

Rogelio Salmona has been the most prominent figure in recent Colombian architecture. His work has given the idea of the house a special dimension, a singular poetic feeling, with a clear sense of place. This sense is set forth, in a synthetic way, in the following statement:

"Differentiating itself from any other form of cultural expression, all architecture is necessarily located in a precise geographical place which is in contact with particular realities. And one cannot demonstrate its qualities without living its space. It so happens that architecture is the only art capable of producing spaces which provoke marvel, evoke, which surprise and enchant"... "Architecture must be a surprise by virtue of its forms and material, for its variety of spaces and use of light and of surroundings. One must be able to

95

Left, One of the basic intentions present in the house is that of helping give form and interest to the space and making each one of its textures felt: brick, wood, glass, plants, and even the transparency of the air which surrounds it.

Bogotá, D.C.

Architect, Herbert Baresch.

discover it, since it is more beautiful to discover by oneself than have it imposed upon one, and when on entering the spaces these produce an evocative and magical effect." [13.]

The Swedish film director Ingmar Bergman once said that he had made only one film... several times. In an analogous way, an architect may conceive, in his mind, one idea about the house which evolves over time. Every work is a development of that house, every moment adds or subtracts elements, allowing him to decipher it from a different point of view. A quick review of the architectures seen in the different houses designed by Rogelio Salmona from the mid-nineteen sixties to the present demonstrates a series of constant values and the appearance of new variables. The diagonal; the search for light through windows, skylights and canopies; the surprising, rather than obvious, communication between spaces; and a particular sense of intimacy are some of the values which have remained constant.

A recurring approach in the domestic architecture of Salmona has been the exploration of the courtyard as a spatial articulator of interior life and the architecture of the dwelling. The management of the patio in the domestic architecture of Salmona restored to the Colombian house one of its archetypal spaces. There were few preceding attempts. [14.] The functionalist house, compressed within its own volume, was conceived as a big box with very large windows to better see the exterior world. The courtyard restored an interiorized external space to the house, adopted for domestic tasks and for contemplation. The patio is the space in which the house looks at itself, in which its enclosures may meet and converse with one another.

The following paragraph of Germán Téllez about the architectural meaning of the House of Distinguished Guests in Cartagena allows one to understand the sense of the succession of patios as a spatial proposal: *"The response of Salmona to the problem set forth was, as it had to be, as complex in its origin and its material expression as in the programmatic and circumstantial parameters established by the project. Although it may be possible that the house in Tabio, in the Sabana of Bogotá, was, chronologically, the predecessor of the house of Distinguished Guests in Cartagena, by virtue of the use of juxtaposed patios as a basic compositional resource, this does not go beyond a conceptual mechanization of a process that was much more simple and direct. The intellectual steps by which Salmona evolved from a savannah house of 500 square metres to another, in Cartagena, of 4,500, cannot be reduced to the comparison of some floor plans which are mistakenly going to show apparent coincidences between the succession of spaces which are closed and opened according to the technical needs of access, illumination and structural support. All this in itself has little importance. What transcends the simple architectural composition is the splendid inspiration with which Salmona manages and creates contiguity among architectural spaces of a very diverse nature. The fundamental feature is the architectural narration which is offered to the inhabitant or observer of the House of Guests, not the hypothetical compositional grammar which may be used to achieve metaphysical ends."* [15.]

From the very beginning, the incursion of Salmona in the handling of domestic space had to do with materials and especially with the use of brick, both for the exterior and the interior. The investigation cannot be reduced to the simple use of a determined material; it is directly focussed on working with the textures which are produced by brick, wood, other natural materials like stone, and concrete, which is generally handled in a brusque way, emphasizing the imperfections resulting from the moulds used in its pouring. In this way profound correlations are established between intentions to relate the interior with the exterior, the interaction of spaces, the seizure of visual effects, and effects of light and work with the textures of the materials employed. The austere use of materials which generally characterizes the architectural work of Salmona is found in his houses, whether they are in the cold atmosphere of Bogotá and its surroundings or in the hot coasts of the Caribbean. Works like the House of Distinguished Guests in Cartagena are now paradigms of Latin American architecture.

The architecture of brick gathered strength in Bogotá as an almost necessary response to the questions of an architecture of place. The Bogotá houses constructed within this idea after 1960 are, to a large extent, its best representatives on a national level. The importance and quality of successive examples served as the basis for a movement of wider coverage in which the common denominator has been a conscious working of the constructional and aesthetic possibilities of ordinary brick. In diverse cities, especially in Medellín, the question of place has been handled with considerable seriousness and an architecture of brick has been experimented with. Young architects like the late Herbert Baresch have contributed their own ideas, with especially interesting results, in a series of houses in which the possibilities of brick and adobe were developed and new spatial concepts were explored as well.

The idea of the house as place is more a matter of feeling than of logic. This feeling has permeated the best domestic architecture in the past thirty years. That which was proposed by Rogelio Salmona in 1959 has become a reality.

Left and above, It is difficult to describe in words the meaning of place in a house. Photography, a mediation of direct experience, draws a more precise portrait of the qualities of space and texture which form part of this meaning. It is the representation of "being there", both without and within.

Bogotá, D.C.
Architect, Rogelio Salmona.

100

Above and right, The art of catching light and drawing it into the interior of the house does not only respond to the practical purposes of natural illumination: it attends to precise aesthetic intentions as well. The qualities of light tinge the places which are constructed and make their spatial intentions evident.

Bogotá, D.C.
Architect, Rogelio Salmona.

Left and above, To create a place —a courtyard or a lobby— goes beyond the physical delimitation of spaces. It has to do with the image of the house and with stimulating the senses through diverse recourses. It also has to do with giving sense to the spaces, making them comprehensible. A patio or a vestibule make sense when a person, as well as understanding, feels it.

Bogotá, D.C.

Architect, Rogelio Salmona.

104

Above and right, The limits of a space may combine precision and ambiguity, in accordance with the position of the observer; it may be clear and, at the same time, create expectations. The diagonal which gives rise to the fire place leads the gaze and the path towards a strip of landscape and light. This gesture is noticeable from a certain point of the room and directs the gaze to the main door.

Bogotá, D.C.
Architect, Rogelio Salmona.

Left and above, Le Corbusier categorically affirmed that architecture is "the wise, correct and magnificent play of volumes beneath light." This play can also be, as in this case, subtle and discreet, suggested, and not necessarily obvious. The personality of each part of the house is perceived when one is near to and wandering by it. When the whole is seen from a distance, the individual units are considered as part of a play of planes, volumes, and textures.

Cartagena, Bolívar.

Architect, Rogelio Salmona.

108

Above and right, The idea of the house consists of a series of suggestions: of forms, of textures, of contrasts, of visual effects, of sequences, and movements. The obvious, that which is caught through a single visual impact, is replaced by a blend of sensations which attract the attention and combine themselves into compositions in which light and shade contribute unsuspected moments. The house invites itself to be known.

Cartagena, Bolívar.
Architect, Rogelio Salmona.

Left and above, The word "texture" indicates the idea of interweaving. By extension, on the perceptual plane, it has become associated with the tactile qualities which arise from the materials, and, in the case of the masonry in stonework, from its bonding. The pictures capture the conjunction of architectural and natural textures. The vegetation is not an isolated detail, it is part of the place.

Cartagena, Bolívar.
Architect, Rogelio Salmona.

113

Left and above, A courtyard is a void which is filled by light, it is also a mass of air. Architecture becomes present to the extent that light falls upon it. The definitive contrast between the solid masses and the voids is accentuated by the shadows which reinforce the techtonic meaning of the pillars, the walls, the stairways and, in general, all fractures of volume. There is a ceremonial sense to the treatment of the whole.

Cota, Cundinamarca.

Architect, Rogelio Salmona.

Following pages, The house evokes, in its forms and spaces, feelings which are solemn and amiable at the same time; it has something of a temple, something of a hamlet, something obvious and something which is insinuated. The walls turn into vaults, form labyrinths and lattices and announce their importance as the builders of the space.

Cota, Cundinamarca.

Architect, Rogelio Salmona.

118

Above and right, The contrasts in the forms and materials of the spaces change their mood. In one case, the inclined, white ceiling draws one's attention and the very space towards the view, while the window receives the impact of this intention. In the other case, the cupola encloses and focuses the attention upon a virtual centre. Here, the window-door is a frame of light and color which animates the austerity of the space.

Bogotá, D.C.

Architect, Hernán Vieco.

Previous pages, The brick, widely employed in Colombia, is made by artisans in the traditional brickworks from wich it takes its name. It accentuates the extreme simplicity and sobriety of the interior spaces of the house.

The space of the covered gallery, with its high enclosed walls and its change of levels, possesses a spirit evocative of the archaic.

Bogotá, D.C.
Architect, Dicken Castro Duque.

Above and right, The house is a space that is useful, not only for family activities, but also to refresh the spirit. The architecture of the house allows itself to be covered with pictures of every size and it discreetly

remains, as a support for this accumulation of images. A beam, a railing, a fragment of wall, announce its presence.

Bogotá, D.C.
Architect, Dicken Castro Duque.

124

Above and right, The small interior courtyard adds to the whole architecture of the house. Everything converges there. The slope of the roof, as well as signalling the importance of the patio. It rises towards openings which create views of the near gardens or the distant mountains. The chromatic uniformity of the materials of the walls, floors, and roof turns a splash of color into a whole event.

Bogotá, D.C.
Architect, Jacques Mosseri.

Left, above and following pages, The intention of the house as place seeks to endow each thing with a special significance within a system of hierarchies which is guided only by the sensibility of the architect. There are no exact rules. The permanent and the accidental have their place within the spaces of the house.

Bogotá, D.C.
Architects, Jorge Rueda, Enrique Gómez, Carlos Morales.

Left and above, The forms of the house are precise and within them the spaces are subdivided in a subtle way. Vertically, three ambits are to be found; that of the furnishing on the floor level; the highest, that of the roof with its wooden structure; and between these, a third, virtual ambit, a void whose role is to provide a definitive scale. The walls show a highly elaborated working both in their contours and in the fissures which form cavities of diverse types and functions. The interior space is contained within an equally precise volume definition.

Chía, Cundinamarca.
Architects, Jorge Rueda,
Carlos Morales.

132

Above and right, an integral example of Bogotá brick architecture with its main elements: a prolix elaboration of the exterior volumes with the strong diagonals created by the pitch of the roofs; the attention given to the texture of common brick both in the exterior and the interior; the working of inlets and projections in the walls and the search for light.

Bogotá, D.C.
Architects, Jorge Rueda,
Carlos Morales.

Left and above, The outside of the house shows all sorts of details which break up its edges and planes and respond to precise intentions about the relation of the interior with its surroundings. The window located at the back of the hall contradicts the tradition of a closed back wall. The precision in the fitting of the window and the masking of its frames creates the illusion of total transparency and introduces nature into the hall.

Bogotá, D.C.
Architects, Jorge Rueda,
Carlos Morales.

Above and right, By being integrated into the spatial system of the house, the stairway adds another component to multidirectionality. Its insinuations and suggestions invite one to go up and down, be still, look, wander.

Going against the idea of a uni-directional space, there are a multitude of architectural events held together by the dominant presence of brick.

Rionegro, Antioquia.
Architect, Oscar Mesa.

138

Above, The archetypal image of the house, set in contemporary language, carries with it a great number of evocations. Each part of the house is worked as a volume with a strong individuality. The unity of the materials of the walls and roofs allow one to perceive these volumes with complete clarity.

Rionegro, Antioquia.
Architect, Oscar Mesa.

139

Above, The inner life, the sense of home, and that which is lived in open spaces, are joined into one image and are revitalized in the experience of the house. The domestic sense of the interior space, within the modern idea, also has to do with images which spring from the collective memory.

Rionegro, Antioquia.
Architect, Oscar Mesa.

140

Above, A house is a set of
sensory stimuli produced by
its architecture, by light, and
by the objects which occupy
or invade it.
To break down the
whole and perceive every
one of its parts demands
alert attention. The
experience of the house
assimilates these stimuli and
converts them into familiar
images.

Medellín, Antioquia.
Architect, Oscar Mesa.

Right, The interior of the
house clearly shows the
balance between the rational
construction of its design and
the interest in interrupting
this rigor with tensions
created by different points of
interest: skylights, doors,
windows, and stairs. The
strong brick elements
accentuate the visual
sensation of the house's
solidity.

Sabaneta, Antioquia.
Architect, Oscar Mesa.

143

Left and above, Adobe, a colonial heritage which is artisanally made and of humble origins, is combined with metal, which is characteristically a standard, mass-produced industrial material. The contrast which arises from this combination turns the house into something which partakes both of the present and the past and is timeless and suggestive.

Ubaté, Cundinamarca.
Architect, Herbert Baresch.

145

Left and above, The stairway stops being an object and becomes a space. The symmetrical —or asymmetrical— resolution of the first flight avoids the conventional image of a stairway and affirms the invitation to go up.

The symmetrical —or asymmetrical —division of the space by means of the window serves as a dividing line between being and watching.

Bogotá, D.C.
Architect, Herbert Baresch.

Left and above, In the historic tradition, the barrel vault has been used for special places: its appearance has a certain solemnity which is transmitted to the space which it covers. The vault direction, inevitably axial, leads the gaze to a point in the distance, in this case the landscape. The lateral openings partly neutralize this axial sense.

Bogotá, D.C.
Architect, Herbert Baresch.

147

149

Left and above, The domestic space is transformed into a reminder of the panelled arab-spanish ornamentation, characteristic of colonial architecture. The appeal of the elaborated roof is joined, as yet another element, to the diverse spatial and tactile experiences of the house.

Bogotá, D.C.

Architect, Herbert Baresch.

Following pages, The space of the stairway covered by the glass canopy is an admirable play of intelligence which combines that which sinks into the earth with that which rises up to the sky in a perfectly-achieved contrast of positive and negative.

Bogotá, D.C.

Architect, Herbert Baresch.

Left and above, The intention of making a house something more than an inhabitable object is seen in the treatment of space and its textures. The details, which are apparently accidental, do not interrupt the sense of domestic life, rather, they are incorporated into it. Specific intentions also exist in the way in which the exterior is dominated and brought towards the interior of the house.

Bogotá, D.C.
Architect, Herbert Baresch.

Following pages, The folds in the brick roof give it structural stability and, at the same time, turn into the main theme of the interior space. The absence of visible supports allows for continuity among the different enclosures defined and characterized by these pleats.

Chocontá, Cundinamarca.
Architect, Herbert Baresch.

153

Left and above, The techtonic, the constructive sense of the house, becomes explicit both in its exterior and in the space contained within the strong volumes. The vertex formed by the two slopes of the roof produces dualisms which are taken special advantage of in the interior. One half is explored, the other is seen.

Chocontá, Cundinamarca.
Architect, Herbert Baresch.

THE ENCOUNTER WITH TRADITION

In August, 1966, the magazine *House Beautiful*, published in New York by the Hearst company, featured various examples of Latin American houses. The choices included the residence of Luis Barragán, a Mexican architect who was not very well known at that time. From Colombia the houses of the architects Enrique Triana and Guillermo Bermúdez, the apartment of the architect Fernando Martínez Sanabria, a house designed by Rafael Obregón and another country house designed by an "amateur" architect, Loli Obregón, were chosen. The magazine singled out, in the last house, the fusion between the modern concept of stories and spaces and the use of traditional materials like log beams, large white-painted plaster walls, and thick, finely cut thatched roofs. The inclusion of this house with the others, representative of diverse ways of understanding modern architecture, may have caused certain anxieties at the time. The incursion of the traditional in the modern was, then, a matter of argument and debate. It no longer is today.

From almost the beginning of the processes of modernization, an interest arose in Colombia about understanding or taking some advantage of Colombian architecture and, especially, colonial heritage, the most akin to the spirit of simplicity and formal schematization characteristic of the rationalist tendencies. The initial modernizing spirit completely rejected any imitative intention and especially, the Neo-Colonial style which had become part of the eclectic spirit which ended the republican era. The presence of the distant past intrigued architects with an avant-garde spirit in the first years of modernization. The feeling of revaluation of the colonial led to some intentional experiments in fusing the modern and the historic. The house was a suitable field for the exploration of this fusion. From this attempt there arose, around 1960, a white domestic architecture, with earthen-tiled roofs, interiors that were also white, exposed wooden beams, and all of this handled within a perfectly modern criterion.

The presence of traditional elements in the architecture of the house necessarily posed a problem of image. The inclined tiled roofs, the white plastering, the wooden carpentering of doors and windows, the floors made up of large ceramic tiles, all of this analogous to that which had been employed in colonial architecture, has the power of evoking it without necessarily imitating it. This was the spirit of the white architecture which has been referred to. The Neo-neocolonial which followed it was based on copying, or

159

Left, The rustic treatment of the exposed roof beams contrasts with the careful working of the wood in the doors and windows. The presence of the sea attracts the direct and indirect gaze of all of the spaces.

Barú, Bolívar.

Architect, Loli Obregón.

parodying, the most obvious, the most colonial gestures. Around 1970 it unleashed a wave of pseudo-colonial houses which were successful among certain social groups because of their traditional appearance.

The Swiss architect Víctor Schmid was a strange personality in the midst of the modernization processes of Colombian architecture. Schmid developed a style of his own in which elements of the Colombian colonial tradition were combined with others derived from the popular architecture of his native country. His houses were characterized by the use of craft materials and artisanal handwork in carpentry, ceramics, and forging. His interest in craftwork led him to design even the smallest details of his houses, which rarely relied upon technical blueprints. Instead he made use of drawings done by his own hand in which he put down his ideas as they evolved in the course of the work. His technical inclinations aside, Schmid was rather skilful in the management of spaces and volumes, which gives value to the architecture of many of his houses.

The traditional house seen through modern eyes has served as the basis for the development, in different regions of the country, of a country house architecture with large straw, palm or tile roofs, whose interior space, with visible timbering, evokes a regional character without necessarily imitating it. The houses designed by Loli Obregón, most of them built in rural areas, show a combination of a spatiality with a modern character and selected features of traditional character. The use of natural materials: wooden logs, straw, palm, plastered and painted walls, and materials with strong textures for the floors, accentuates this attempt to fuse the new and the traditional. An interest in views which result from the site, and functional considerations help to emphasize the settling of the house into its site and, if we may put it this way, its rootedness.

The interest in constructional forms and techniques developed on the basis of a study of materials belonging to regional and local traditions, is considerably more recent and is framed within an attitude of innovation. The rationalization of the handling of materials like wood and bamboo, strongly rooted in the cultures of some regions of the country, has allowed for the creation of new sources of technological and architectural inspiration. The work of architects like Marcelo Villegas and Simón Vélez, whose interest in the subject of the house led them into their own special explorations, is representative of this line of thought. Wood and bamboo, their favorite materials, are worked, without obvious references to traditional architecture, in bold forms and structures which stretch their constructional possibilities to the limit and at the same time create a unique aesthetic idea.

Darío Ruiz Gómez refers to the architecture of Simón Vélez in the following way:

"The use of materials like mangrove and bamboo does not represent, in Simón Vélez, a lyrical nostalgia for nature but rather a veiled philosophy of life in which, through these materials, a resistance to any form of technological rationalism is made evident. Here [...] the feeling of what is primitive responds to a need to introduce, to the terrain of human experience, a series of sensations which that rationalism had been eliminating with its one-dimensional vision of life. The preserved purity of the quality, the smell of a given wood are, above all, pure images of that forgotten world, of that former world which has been ignominiously demolished for being thought of as unproductive 'nature'." [16]

Francisco Ramírez, for his part, adds the following appraisal:

"Vélez injects new significance into the basic formulations of the regional constructional culture. He renounces the attempt to revitalize previous forms, approaching tradition in an original way, avoiding the repetition of merely superficial effects. His synthesis operates at an intense level, without attempting to forge constructional traditions with universal forms of composition and distribution. He has sought to give more strength to a particular way of constructing. By condensing place and living, construction and landscape, he arrives at the deed of construction through a very lucid cultural point of view." [17]

The architecture of the houses of Simón Vélez is not only an exercise in notable structures. One of his main concerns is the setting forth of different proposals for the relation between the interior and the exterior, some direct, others elaborated through the textures and transparencies produced by intricate and subtle ways of handling wood, bamboo or poles of chonta-palm wood. His country houses may be read as big covered exterior spaces or as enormous open interior ones.

The Colombian architectural tradition offers many areas for a task of appraisal and of synthesis. The work conceived in the spirit of an encounter with tradition cannot easily be classified within the categories of rationalist and organicist, of abstractionist or architecture of place. They form a special territory of confluence in which the modern spirit intercedes in that which arises from the historic or the vernacular in order to achieve different but, in the end, modern results.

163

Left and above, The artisanal fabrication of the house is derived from local and European traditions. The visual composition of the spaces and their interrelations obey modern ideas. In the midst of the great quantity of carefully elaborated ideas some traces of abstraction are found, especially in the handling of the geometry of the forms.

Bogotá, D.C.
Architect, Víctor Schmid.

164

Above and right, The architect has skilfully managed the old and the new in the space of the lobby.
All of the details are elaborated with an especially careful sense of manual work which combines refinement with a sense of the rustic. The architect's hand is also seen in the fabrication of furniture and objects.

Bogotá, D.C.
Architect, Víctor Schmid.

Left and above, The proportion of the space is given by the form and inclination of the roof. It looks important and comfortable at the same time. The view takes on all of its importance. The transparency of the window in the background softens the strong presence of the trunks in the roof. The composition of the lines and horizontal planes in another enclosure are broken by the curved mouth of the fireplace, the only sign of imperfection in the whole. The liking for artisanal materials in the furnishing reinforces the presence of tradition in the house.

Sabana de Bogotá.
Architect, Loli Obregón.

167

168

Above and right, The form and
material of the roof is based
on the traditional
architecture of the region.
The handling of the big
windows which break the
walls derives from the
modern idea of an
integration between the
interior and the surrounding
environs. This is one of the
ways that the coming and
going between the traditional
and modern becomes
apparent.

Sabana de Bogotá.
Architect, Loli Obregón.

Above and right, The lines in the wood of the floor divisions and roofs stand out, by contrast, with the white surfaces of the walls and the ceilings. The openings are towards the setting and their forms follow intentions to widen or restrict the fragments of landscape introduced into the house.

Sabana de Bogotá.
Architect, Loli Obregón.

172

Above, In enclosures stripped of furniture architectural values are clearly shown. Beyond the artisanal work and possible references to the traditional, what stands out is a sense of synthesis which inscribes the language of the house within the principle of "less is more".

Sabana de Bogotá.
Architect, Loli Obregón.

173

Above, The working of solid mass is incorporated in the play of dark lines and white surfaces the main subject of the house design. References to a specific tradition are diluted in a much broader concept of what the idea of the traditional or of the modern may mean.

Sabana de Bogotá.
Architect, Loli Obregón.

Following pages, The image of the "cottage", the English country dwelling which was such a favorite in the country architecture of the Bogotá savannah during the nineteen thirties and forties, is revived in this house. The arms extend over the terrain in order to bring the interior enclosures closer to the landscape.

Chía, Cundinamarca.
Architect, Pablo Sanín.

176

Above and right, This virtuoso work begins with the selection of the kinds of wood needed for combining the densities and colorings. It continues with the fabrication of the structure of the house, especially the roof, whose lines indicate the directions of the wood. The interior space has something of a ship and something of a cathedral. The window, almost in the air, throws itself into the immensity of the distant landscape.

Manizales, Caldas.

Architect, Marcelo Villegas.

Above, The façade, covered with metallic sheets, revives a technique employed in the past in the city, named the "metallic plaster wall" by historian Jorge Enrique Robledo. The visible structure of wood is drawn over the metal background.

Manizales, Caldas.
Architect, Marcelo Villegas.

Right, The house is perched over a reef. Its figure evokes that of a bird in repose. The bold structural design is the protagonist of the house and is hardly veiled by the wooden shutters which protect its interior.

Rosario islands, Bolívar.
Architect, Simón Vélez.

Left and above, The encounter with tradition revives the visual and spatial importance of the roof and especially, of its structure, which is visible in all the spaces. The diagonal and perpendicular lines of the wood, inserted into the walls or loose and articulated in the arches, are the directional points of the house spaces. They are perceived as part of the whole scheme of support and detail of the house.

Cali, Valle del Cauca.
Architect, Simón Vélez.

182

Above, right and following pages, It may seem redundant to put into words what these images say about the structural and aesthetic sense of work with wooden trunks. This aesthetic of the structural derives from the modern schematic treatment of the system of columns and beams and also derives from the simple artisanal work based on tradition. By virtue of its design it may be thought of as something which is special and its own, its value lies, in the way that a structure is conceived, the structure by its mere presence, creates the space and makes the house.

La Pintada, Antioquia.
Architect, Simón Vélez.

186

Above and right, Building in wood imposes its own rules on the space of the house and forms the linear systems which inscribe both a white wall and a distant view. The repertory employed includes diverse forms of wood: trunks, rods, polished surfaces, and carved pieces. The house is a master class in the subject.

Manizales, Caldas.
Architect, Simón Vélez.

188

Above, Bamboo, mainly employed in the popular housing of the coffee-growing region in the centre of the country, is submitted here to a different idea of structural and aesthetic behaviour. The large, crossed sheaves of bamboo poles take on the role of pillars for the house.

The treatment of the different lengths of some poles, which stick out on the outside and recede within, transforms the beams into aesthetically active elements and cancels out their apparent rigidity.

Manizales, Caldas.
Architect, Simón Vélez.

189

Above, The covered porch and gable-end, characteristic of the traditional architectural of the central coffee-growing region, are fused here in a single space whose roof is supported by enormous projecting parts from the bamboo structure. By virtue of its size and proportions, this space lends itself both to socializing and the simple contemplation of the landscape.

Manizales, Caldas.
Architect, Simón Vélez.

Following pages, The impressive structure of the house, built in bamboo, resembles that of a hangar. As well as displaying great imagination and an obvious technical virtuosity, a completely new and distinct idea of a country house is set forth here.

Manizales, Caldas.
Architect, Simón Vélez.

THE MODERN AS THE PRESENT

In the last paragraph of the *Historia de la arquitectura en Colombia,* by the architect Silvia Arango, appears the following:

"Any reader who is familiar with the contemporary conceptual universe will recognize, in current Colombian proposals, ideological similarities to developments in other parts of the world. What is promising and original in Colombian architecture is its having taken advantage of a tradition of conscious assimilation which allows one to harness general realities on the basis of specific situations, and having had persons with enough talent to be able to shape them with the necessary quality."[18.]

The word "modern", in its remote origin, meant the new and also the up-to-date. This second sense upholds the validity of the modern, even in epochs of scepticism and crisis such as post-modernity. The tradition of the new demands a constant revision and bringing up to date: it cannot remain as it is, it must transform itself. Therefore it is relevant to ask, Are the rationalist and functionalist postulates still valid? Does the architecture of place still make sense? Is it a characteristic of the young to understand and appreciate the architecture which surrounds it?

The architect has today an available field of references and influences much wider than that which existed fifty years ago, when the modernizing influence began to make itself felt, and even that available thirty years ago, when the organicist secession began in Bogotá architecture. There exist diverse tendencies of what is called post-modernity, Contextualism and its various interpretations, the Deconstructionist movement, which has been proposed as the contemporary avant-garde, without leaving aside a critical look at the modern and an equally critical look at the conceptual and practical course of modern Colombian architecture. The scenario is more complex and demands more knowledge and thought.

A particularly satisfying aspect of this process has been the discovery of modern Latin American architecture through the works of its great masters. This discovery has led to the appraisal of work which was ignored for decades and has given a basis to the systematic study of modernity in each country. Paradigmatic figures like the Mexican architect, Luis Barragán, the Venezuelan Carlos Raúl Villanueva, the Brazilians Lucio Costa and Oscar Niemeyer and the recognition given to the work of contemporary architects like Rogelio Salmona, Severiano Porto, Juvenal Baracco, Jesús Tenreiro, and Eladio Dieste, among others, have become models to follow, or imitate, in recent architecture. *"The appearance of the Spanish edition of the book by Charles Jencks, 'The language of post-modern architecture' (G.*

Left, The rhythm set by the steps of the stairway is adopted as a guideline for establishing, with the windows, the rhythm of the porch, whose distant end indicates the interest in the axial approach seen in the inside of the house.

Bogotá, D.C.
Architect, Billy Escobar.

Gili, Barcelona, 1980) not only gave wide circulation to the term but also to a type of architecture which moved away from the aesthetic models of the modern movement. Apart from the superficiality of the text and the fact that many of the examples given were no longer very valid, it helped in Latin America (apart from enabling some of commercial architecture to appropriate a large part of the historical repertory of the architecture that was presented as post-modern) to enable us to see how the orthodoxy of functionalist rationalism had been revised in the leading countries, which allowed for a look at those architectures which had developed along other aesthetic and technical paths. The decade of the eighties would see new statements arise which, not only in architecture but in culture in general, demonstrated the crisis of modernity, raising the possibility, along the way, of a new stage or a profound revision of it but also allowing for its possible continuance. Since the nineteen eighties the modernity - postmodernity debate has become highly important, giving way to an intense questioning which also affects the revision of the relation between the center and the periphery; its implications in cultural developments; the meaning of the avant-garde movements themselves; the role of technique, ideas about development, the city and public space as heritage and architecture, etc. In this way more room was given to the importance of the debate about Latin American architecture." [19.]

In the above quotation, Francisco Ramírez summarizes, in a highly precise way, some of the important changes which have recently come about in the idea and realization of architecture in Latin America. From a certain point in recent time, the debate about the validity of modern architecture and the conviction that we are on the threshold of a new era, has come to hold the attention not only of architects but also of practically everyone interested in world affairs. Paradoxicallly it has also revived the interest in the modern and, above all, in the authenticity of its fundamental principles. The modern has not only disappeared but it is also being revised, purified, revived and revindicated daily.

This attitude continues, to a certain extent, to sustain an exploration of the possibilities of the modern spirit of the house, but it contributes to it a much stronger and more conscious regional or local meaning, supported on many occasions by historical and critical studies of and research into the characteristic architecture of each site. Architects of different generations have designed and built houses in which elements of modernity and of place are consciously handled within contemporary conceptual schemes. Among others, we might name Laureano Forero, Oscar Mesa, Patricia Gómez, Santiago Caicedo, Jorge Mario Gómez, and Alejandro Echeverri in

Medellín, Jaime Vélez and Benjamín Barney in Cali, and Luis Manuel Briceño, Carlos Campuzano, Luis Kopec, Luis Restrepo, and José María Rodríguez in Bogotá. This group demonstrates some outstanding proposals of Colombian professional work during the past twenty years.

At the present moment a number of conceptual confrontations are to be seen amongst the different alternatives which the architect is asked to judge upon. To be up-to-date means, for many, to be in fashion and this is interpreted as a rejection of what is already established. Abstraction, the idea of place and a look at tradition, confront international fashions and the challenge is to decide which is best and what must be done. The most representative achievements of the modern Colombian house have been incorporated among the totality of attractive alternatives. The architect is faced with the necessity to chose what his position should be with regard to architecture and the subject of the house.

A common denominator of recent architecture is the idea of the house as an object which is aesthetically conceived. This aestheticism allows for an emphasis on all which has previously been elaborated in the architecture of the modern house: form and space, texture, and place. In the modern fashion, the new house-object is seen as a volume or play of volumes which contain habitable spaces. This volume is placed in the landscape in order to be appreciated and appraised, from outside, as an architectural exercise full of subtle intellectual gestures and, from within, as a movement of diverse sensations. The preference for pure forms, alone or in combination, or the complex work of interwoven volumes, allows for the creation of objects which must, above all, be beautiful, even when one is guilty, at times, of pretentiousness. The use of virtual elements lends interest to the reading of the house. The formal attraction which characterizes this idea of architecture is evident in many of the new houses built in recent years on the outskirts of big cities and in the tourist condominiums which have proliferated throughout the Colombian countryside. To all of this is added another element, color, which contrasts with the austerity of brick architecture and which accentuates the value of forms often conceived within a rigorous purism.

This architecture, whose intentions are sustained by the discourse characteristic of the present time, is being enthusiastically developed by young professionals whose ideas challenge established ones, welcome them, transform them or replace them with others. The return to abstraction, as part of a new look at modernity, appears, today, to be closing a circle that was opened five decades ago.

Previous pages, At dusk the apertures of the house are seen as large mouths destined to catch air and coolness and carry them into the interior spaces. The volumes stand out sharply against the sky, forming a silhouette that is impossible to capture at any other moment.

Ricaurte, Cundinamarca.
Architect, Jorge Pérez Norzagaray.

Above and right, The house is a whole exercise in geometric forms both in the volume and in the surfaces and openings. The colors employed –yellow, blue and white– form part of a study, strict and happy at the same time, of its rural character.

Nilo, Cundinamarca.
Architect, Enrique Triana Uribe.

200

Above and right, According to a visitor, the house is "tied up by light". In turn, the space of the living room is seen to be tied up by the books which cover the walls.

The fireplace and the stairway intrude in it.

Chía, Cundinamarca.
Architects, Alberto Saldarriaga,
Rodrigo Rubio.

Left and above, The intentional use of elements of architecture from the past in the modern space of the house is not only limited to such details as the moulding of the hall roof or the republican door in the gallery. Forms and proportions, thresholds and axial senses are revived. The house has a sense of the nostalgic.

Envigado, Antioquia.

Architect, Alvaro Barrera.

206

Previous pages, The diverse stylistic references which form part of the architectural language of the house are incorporated in a succession of spaces in which the thresholds assume a special importance. This recuperation of the threshold brought, to domestic architecture, a feature that was important for the special quality of the traditional house. The materials and their textures complement the agreeable character of the interior of the house.

Suesca, Cundinamarca.
Architect, Felipe Londoño.

Above, The architecture of the savannah country house is evoked and re-created both in the external forms and interior spaces. Details, especially the cornices, are treated as architectural themes which, joined to the handling of color, give character to the image of the house.

Suesca, Cundinamarca.
Architect, Felipe Londoño.

207

Above, The structure of the exposed roof and the treatment of the fireplace emphasize reminiscences of the traditional in the inside of the house. The large window, with its uninterrupted transparency, plays the role of a big picture full of nature.

Suesca, Cundinamarca.
Architect, Felipe Londoño.

Left and above, The rude handling of the volumes of concrete on the outside of the house contrasts with the polished working of the surfaces in the interior. The abundant vegetation incorporated into the architecture receives natural light through skylights of different shapes which are integrated into the general composition of the space.

Bogotá, D.C.
Architect, Luis Kopec.

210

Right, The language of the house's interior architecture revives elements from the purist period of modern architecture but its handling is completely contemporary and shows clear aesthetic intentions in the subdivision of the plane of the façade into two strips, one solid and the other transparent, and the floating appearance of the second storey balcony.

Bogotá, D.C.
Architect, Luis Kopec.

212

Above and right, The glass canopy, one of the relatively recent contributions to the interior design of the house, is worked as an important part of its specialness. The lines formed by its supports find an echo in the lines of the wood of the ceiling. The effect of floating volume is repeated in the treatment of the stairway.

Bogotá, D.C.

Architect, Luis Kopec.

Left and above, The main volume is brought out in an obvious way. Its cubic form, the material and the color of the faces distinguish it from the rest of the house, with its large stone walls and ridged texture. A geometric turn of the cube provides space for the different ambits of the place without neglecting the importance of the axial composition of the main apertures.

Anapoima, Cundinamarca.
Architect, Luis Kopec.

218

Previous pages, The spirit of the traditional urban house of the Valley of Cauca is present here. Nevertheless, the architectural elements of these two houses are strictly modern and are worked in such a way that they cannot be labelled as simple references.

The play of light and shadow makes this quality even more evident.

Cali, Valle del Cauca.
Architect, Benjamín Barney Caldas.

Above and right, The intention of sobriety in the interior of the house, which shows itself in the supremacy of white, allows for the definition of the value of the volumes formed by the walls and exalts the presence of railings, inserts and projections in the manner of unfolded planes which form spaces of different dimensions. The white also creates a luminosity which catches the light of the windows and diffuses it throughout the interior. The treatment of the window is interesting. The transparent strip only attends to the branches of the eucalyptuses. The rest is a mere matter of illumination.

Bogotá, D.C.
Architect, Hernando Vargas Caicedo.

Left and above, In the broad and almost empty space, the railing stands out as just another sculptured form, but its geometry is different. A detailed observation of the pictures enables one to appreciate subtle intentions in the handling of the form, space, and light, which, in the end, is what allows for the definition of individual forms and the creation of the diverse shades of their perception.

Bogotá, D.C.
Architect, Hernando Vargas Caicedo.

221

223

Left, The fabrics which sieve the light through the skylight, form a virtual limit, change the proportions of the space, and give value to the view over the garden. The diffuse light which is reflected in the the white surfaces of the walls and floor makes the room a special place.

Nocaima, Cundinamarca.
Architect, Luis Tamayo.

Above, Every detail worked in the volume of the house corresponds to a detail in its interior, whose façade is folded in order to form spaces of different kinds and functions and delimit one or another fragment of the landscape of the lake. The light breaks into the interior, in a definitive way, through the skylight.

Sesquilé, Cundinamarca.
Architect, Rafael Obregón Herrera.

225

Left, above and following pages, Spatial ideas in the house, such as the central courtyard and the inclined roofs which converge on it, are joined and reworked with a new treatment of materials and details. The textured brick masses are worked with a certain virtuosity which accentuates the contrasts of light and shade. In the interior there is a return to the austerity of large white surfaces.

Bogotá, D.C.
Architect, Carlos Campuzano.

230

Above and right, In the house contemporary elaborations of elements from the past are found, such as the patio and the wooden structure of the roof. In the singular working of the fireplace the abstract structure of the composition is seen, as well as the modified role of the brick texture, which gives a new personality to the whole.

Bogotá, D.C.
Architect, Billy Escobar.

Above and right, The fragmentation of the house, which is due not only to topographic factors but also to an architectural idea, is made evident both in the directions of the vaults and in the multiplicity of visual angles which are displayed from a certain viewpoint. This fragmentation makes the experience of the house to unite diverse sensations when one is in a room or wandering through it. The white surfaces, framed by brick borders, stand out as contrasting planes in the texture of the interior space.

Tenjo, Cundinamarca.
Architects, Willem Goebertus,
Catalina Mariño.

Previous pages, The illuminated house is a showcase which demonstrates the contents of its interior and its uninterrupted relation with the exterior. A reading of the internal space allows for an appreciation of the intention of visual and spatial continuity of the different ambits.

Amagá, Antioquia.
Architect, Laureano Forero.

Above and right, The sobriety of the forms of the exterior volumes and of the internal space is softened with traditional touches, mouldings, and carvings, in a play characteristic of the present freedom given to the aesthetic handling of the house.

Pereira, Risaralda.
Architect, Laureano Forero.

238

The dark coloring of the interior, derived from the abundant presence of wood helps to bring out the visual and color values of the pictures and of the light which is caught through the apertures. There is an intention of axiality in the spaces, indicated by the vertex of the roof structure.

Above, Medellín, Antioquia.
Architects, Santiago Caicedo, Patricia Gómez.

Right, La Fe, Antioquia.
Architect, Jorge Mario Gómez.

242

Previous pages, Two houses and two architects show similar intentions in the handling of the interior space: vertical and horizontal integration and spatial moves that are achieved through the management of planes and volumes. In one house, monochromatic treatment and smooth textures are favored. In the other, the handling of stronger colors and textures is preferred.

Left, Cali, Valle del Cauca. Architect, Jaime Vélez.

Right, Cali, Valle del Cauca. Architect, Luis Fernando Zúñiga.

The pictures capture the different spatial effects of the forms assumed by the roofs in each house. In one of them, the inclination of the planes increases the opening of the spaces towards the outside through a centrifugal effect. In the other, the four-angled roof and the design of the structure emphasize the idea of center. The treatment of the wood is also different. The use of color in the structure of the roof makes the wood, as such, disappear and, through the contrast with the background, brings out the formal value of its lines.

Above, El Peñol, Antioquia. Architects, Santiago Caicedo, Patricia Gómez.

Right, Medellín, Antioquia. Architects, Santiago Caicedo, Patricia Gómez.

Left and above, The form and working of the roof, whose rising spiral terminates in an edge of light, defines different scales in the space which it covers. The dynamic character imprinted by the combination of the curve and the rise in height, leads gaze and movement towards a complex intersection of forms.

Envigado, Antioquia.
Architects, Alejandro Echeverri,
Juan Bernardo Echeverri.

248

Previous pages, Similar intentions are seen in two different houses.
The wooden beams which serve to support the floor divisions and roofs are worked as guidelines for the interior spatial concept. Horizontal or inclined, parallel or oblique, they give rhythm and direction and unite their texture to the others which are joined in each enclosure.

La Fe, Antioquia.
Architects, Alejandro Echeverri, Juan Bernardo Echeverri

Above and right, One intention, that of the integration and interaction of spaces by means of voids, forms part of an attitude which has remained constant in some approaches to the subject of the house.
Another intention which may be seen is that of turning the near or distant views into aesthetically-worked motifs through the form and dimensions of the windows.

Bogotá, D.C.
Architect, Daniel Bermúdez Samper.

Left and above, The importance given to the roof as the shaper and main actor of the space is seen in these houses. Nevertheless, the results are different, in scale and proportion and in the character which is achieved by means of the reduction or increase of the walls and the finishes used in them.

Chía, Cundinamarca.
Architect, Juan Manuel Restrepo.

Following pages, The separated porch of the house is a pretext for the elaboration of geometrical effects with the vertical supports and the horizontal elements of the pergola and the floor plans. It is also a pretext to break that geometry with the natural curve of a hammock.

Anapoima, Cundinamarca.
Architect, Mónica Gómez de Espinosa.

254

Above and right, The theory of white on white applied to the outside and inside of the house is characteristic of an architectural idea inspired by contemporary rationalism. The small exception of color is introduced as a contrasting element without altering the dominant monochromatic quality.

Anapoima, Cundinamarca.
Architect, Alberto Valovis.

257

Left and above, The play of contrasts, intelligently set forth and resolved, between the modern idea of space and form and a roof which recuperates the forms and materials of the local tradition, results in a simple and evocative space. The handling of the openings ensures a free interchange between the interior and the exterior and frames fragments of the surrounding landscape with vertical or horizontal strips.

Nilo, Cundinamarca.
Architect, Carlos Felipe Botero.

260

Previous pages, above and right, The architecture of the house is decidedly modern. The clear and direct way in which the forms are worked, the supremacy of white and the handling of the lines formed by the metallic and wooden carpentry indicate affinities with the aesthetics of the abstract.
A red plane, with its chromatic vibration, breaks into the serenity of the inside of the house.

Bogotá, D.C.

Architect, Luis Restrepo.

Above and right, Brick has been employed in different ways in the architecture of Bogotá and its surrounding area. Here it is expressed in geometrically-precise bodies. The linear character of the house is indicated by a continuous horizontal which unites the edges of the volumes. The fireplaces and roofs stand out as superimposed prisms, whose definition is equally precise.

Subachoque, Cundinamarca.
Architect, Luis Restrepo.

264

Right, The spatial unity of the interior of the house is achieved by means of a skilful working of the roof planes which tally with the changes of direction in the ground plan. The entrances of light add clarity to a space which is luminous in itself.

The view of the living room is prolonged through the consevatory, which acts as a solar heater that benefits the climate of the interior.

Subachoque, Cundinamarca.
Architect, Luis Restrepo.

268

Previous pages, A porch-
bridge, the joining element of
the house, allows for the
shaping of spaces of different
heights and their integration
into a sequence. The white
color applied to the surfaces
built in cement blocks
softens their
texture without altogether
losing it.

Girardot, Cundinamarca.
Architect, Luis Manuel Briceño.

Above and right, In the
portico-gallery which runs
around the front of the
house, a much-lauded feature
of traditional country
architecture is found. The
materials employed in the
inside and outside of the
house —ceramics, wood,
white or colored plaster— are
also typical of the traditional
culture. Although their
handling and composition are
devoid of any explicit
references to the past, they
still have the power to
transmit the character of the
country house.

La Pradera, Cundinamarca.
Architects, José María Rodríguez,
Ivonne Valencia.

271

Left and above, The house is an abstract sculpture made of masonry. Each volume is clearly distinguished from the rest. Each aperture reveals the character of the spaces which it shelters in the interior.

The ridged texture of the inner and outer surfaces is brought out by contact with the light.

Tocaima, Cundinamarca. Architects, José María Rodríguez, Ivonne Valencia.

Left and above, The sequence of the spaces opened towards the exterior is communicated by the circulation which borders them. The solid masonry shapes the pilasters, hollows and platforms which serve as furnishings. The house is also a question of light and of diverse shadows, some dense, some muted. With them, diverse climactic textures are established.

Tocaima, Cundinamarca.
Architects, José María Rodríguez,
Ivonne Valencia.

EPILOGUE

Will there ever be a last modern house? Its hypothetical appearance will mark the end of another era and the beginning of one that is even more unpredictable. One does not know if there will ever be a futuristic house.

The house is a species in danger of extinction. As we approach the end of the twentieth century an urbanized humanity tends ever more to live in large, dense urban concentrations where apartment buildings predominate. The house is still a privilege which, paradoxically, only the very rich and the poor enjoy. Country houses, week-end houses, are often alternatives for people who close themselves into their apartments during the week –surrounded on all sides by neighbors– and who look to the countryside for the experience of living in a house.

Throughout this century, the modern Colombian house has returned to that condition of objectivity which guided the architecture of the earliest examples built sixty years ago. In the beginning, the house was a "machine" or an abstract object of art: today it may be a sculpture, a beautiful object placed in the landscape in order to be seen and appreciated from certain distances. Between these two objective approaches we find the other, that of the house as place, guided by a particular sensibility, an existential one, which gives it spirit, and animates it. All of this finds shelter beneath the multi-layered cloak of a modernity which, despite seeming obvious and precise, continues to be enigmatic.

In Colombia, during the last decade, we have seen a boom in domestic construction and especially, of suburban houses. At the same time, the city centres have been dense with enormous apartment buildings. The boom of the house, in present circumstances, may be the swan song for a way of living that may be on the point of a forced disappearance. Or, on the other hand, it may be a confirmation of the validity of a form of habitation which was born at the dawn of a human culture and will endure as long as that culture exists.

The first modern houses were conceived of as part of a radical change in the ways of life. They tested the determination of the architects who, in defiance of traditionalist movements, imposed their ideas. These houses are already part of the past of Colombian architecture: nowadays many are only memories that have been preserved in drawings and photos. Progress, seen as a race to keep up with the new, has passed over those houses which were once the unmistakeable emblem of progress. The modern may be as ephimeral as the past.

277

Previous pages, The image of the house with its barely insinuated forms and its illuminated rooms, open towards the shadows of the night, perfectly captures the ancestral sense of refuge and of home.

Tunja, Boyacá.

Architects, José María Rodríguez, Ivonne Valencia.

FOOTNOTES

1. BERGER, Peter et al. *The homeless mind.* Penguin, Middlesex, 1970.

2. BERMAN, Marshall. *Todo lo sólido desvanece en el aire.* Siglo XXI, México, 1989. p. 1.

3. PARRA, Lisímaco. "Modernidad y ciencia", in AA.VV. *Estructura científica y desarrollo social.* Misión de Ciencia y Tecnología, Fonade, Bogotá, 1990, p. 564.

4. GARCIA CANCLINI, Néstor. *Las culturas híbridas.* Grijalbo, México, 1990, p. 13.

5. ORTEGA, Alfredo. *La arquitectura de Bogotá.* (1924). Ediciones Proa Bogotá, 1988, p. 74.

6. ARANGO, Jorge and MARTINEZ, Carlos. *Arquitectura en Colombia.* Ediciones Proa, Bogotá, 1951, p. 32.

7. MARTINEZ, Carlos. *Arquitectura en Colombia.* Ediciones Proa, Bogotá, 1963, p. 13.

8. TELLEZ, Germán. "La arquitectura y el urbanismo en la época actual. 1935 a 1979". In AA. VV. *Manual de Historia de Colombia,* Volume III. Instituto Colombiano de Cultura, Bogotá, 1979, p. 367.

9. SALMONA, Rogelio. "Notas sugeridas por un proyecto." In *Revista Proa,* No. 127, Bogotá, 1959.

10. ARANGO, Silvia. *Historia de la arquitectura en Colombia.* Universidad Nacional, Bogotá, 1989, pp. 237-238.

11. TELLEZ, Germán. "Perfil de un arquitecto". In *Crítica e imagen.* Escala, Bogotá. n.d, p. 245.

12. MONTENEGRO, Fernando and NIÑO, Carlos. *La vivienda de Guillermo Bermúdez.* Escala, Bogotá, n.d., p. 15.

13. SALMONA, Rogelio. "Consideraciones sobre la arquitectura latinoamericana", in *Revista Proa* No. 318. Bogotá, May, 1983, p. 15.

14. A house in El Poblado, Medellín, built in 1966, may be considered as the first in which Salmona dealt with the subject of the patio. See *Monografía Proa* No. 3, Bogotá, 1990.

15. TELLEZ, Germán. *Rogelio Salmona. Arquitectura y poética del lugar.* Escala, Bogotá, 1991, pp. 282-283.

16. RUIZ GOMEZ, Darío. "La arquitectura de Simón Vélez: La lógica de lo primitivo". In *Simón Vélez. Un sentido de lo construido.* Cámara de Comercio, Cali, n.d.

17. RAMIREZ POTES, Francisco. "Simón Vélez: Un sentido de construir". In *Simón Vélez. Un sentido de lo construido.* Cámara de Comercio, Cali, n.d.

18. ARANGO, Silvia. *Historia de la arquitectura en Colombia.* Universidad nacional, Bogotá, 1989, p. 273.

19. RAMIREZ, Francisco. "Una mirada a la generación de los ochenta". In *Revista Proa* No, 425, Bogotá, June, 1995, p. 54.

BIBLIOGRAPHY

ARANGO, Silvia. "Tendencias actuales de la arquitectura en Colombia." In *Arte en Colombia* No. 17, Bogotá, 1981.

ARANGO, Silvia. *Historia de la arquitectura en Colombia.* Universidad Nacional, Bogotá, 1989.

ARANGO, Silvia. "Notas sobre tres casas de Rogelio Salmona". In: *Rogelio Salmona. Monografía Proa* No. 3. Ediciones Proa, Bogotá, 1990.

ARANGO, Silvia. "Modos de actuar, sentir y pensar en la arquitectura moderna latinoamericana". In *Revista Proa* No. 407, Bogotá, November, 1991.

ARANGO, Jorge and MARTINEZ, Carlos. *Arquitectura en Colombia.* Ediciones Proa, Bogotá, 1951.

FONSECA, Lorenzo and SALDARRIAGA, Alberto. *Aspectos de la arquitectura contemporánea en Colombia.* Editorial Colina, Medellín, 1977.

MARTINEZ, Carlos. *Arquitectura en Colombia.* Ediciones Proa, Bogotá, 1984.

MONTENEGRO, Fernando and NIÑO, Carlos. *Fernando Martínez Sanabria. Trabajos de arquitectura,* n.d. Escala, Bogotá.

MONTENEGRO, Fernando and NIÑO, Carlos. *La vivienda de Guillermo Bermúdez.* Escala, Bogotá, n.d.

ORTEGA, Alfredo. *Arquitectura de Bogotá.* Ediciones Proa, Bogotá, 1988.

RAMIREZ POTES, Francisco. "La casa moderna en Cali". In *La casa en la arquitectura moderna colombiana.* Exhibition catalogue, Cámara de Comercio, Cali, 1990.

RUIZ, Dario. "La casa moderna en Medellín". In *La casa en la arquitectura moderna colombiana.* Exhibition catalogue, Cámara de Comercio, Cali, 1990.

SALDARRIAGA, Alberto. *Arquitectura y cultura en Colombia.* Universidad Nacional, Bogotá, 1986.

TELLEZ, Germán. *Crítica e imagen.* Escala, Bogotá, n.d.

TELLEZ, Germán. "Urbanismo y arquitectura en la época actual. 1935 a 1979". In AA. VV. *Manual de Historia de Colombia,* Volume III. Instituto Colombiano de Cultura, Bogotá, 1979.

TELLEZ, Germán. *Rogelio Salmona. Arquitectura y poética del lugar.* Escala, Bogotá, 1991.